DO YOU KNOW

The Rhinoceros?

Written by
Alain M. Bergeron
Michel Quintin
Sampar

Illustrations by
Sampar

Translated by
Solange Messier

Fitzhenry & Whiteside

First published as "Savais-Tu? Les Rhinocéros" by Editions Michel Quintin, Québec, Canada, J0E 2N0
Published in Canada by Fitzhenry & Whiteside, 195 Allstate Parkway, Markham, Ontario L3R 4T8
Published in the United States by Fitzhenry & Whiteside, 311 Washington Street, Brighton, Massachusetts 02135

10 9 8 7 6 5 4 3 2 1

Library and Archives Canada Cataloguing in Publication
Do You Know Rhinoceros?
ISBN 978-1-55455-354-9 (pbk.)
Data available on file

Publisher Cataloging-in-Publication Data (U.S.)
Do You Know Rhinoceros?
ISBN 978-1-55455-354-9
Data available on file

Fitzhenry & Whiteside acknowledges with thanks the Canada Council for the Arts, and the Ontario Arts Council for their support of our publishing program. We acknowledge the financial support of the Government of Canada through the Canada Book Fund (CBF) for our publishing activities.

Cover and text design by Daniel Choi
Cover image by Sampar

Printed in China

There are five **species** of rhinoceros. Two of those—the white rhinoceros and black rhinoceros—live in Africa. The other three species live in Asia.

You have no choice. I always take blacks.

This **mammal** is the only animal on Earth with a horn on its nose. The name rhinoceros is derived from Greek words that signify "nose" and "horn."

The black rhinoceros, the white rhinoceros, and the Sumatran rhinoceros all possess two horns. The Indian rhinoceros and the Javan rhinoceros only possess one.

The record for the longest horn is held by a white rhinoceros. Its horn was 1.66 metres (5.4 feet) long. By comparison, that's the height of the average woman.

A rhinoceros' horn determines its rank among the other rhinoceros.

When two rhinoceros meet, they cross their horns like fencers crossing swords. They do this in order to test each other's strength and reflexes.

A broken horn will regrow in two to three years. Just like our nails and hair, a rhinoceros' horn is made of **keratin**.

You took your bath *before* going to sleep? What were you thinking!?

Rhinoceros bathe in mud in order to cool off and also to protect themselves from bug bites.

The black rhinoceros isn't actually black, and the white rhinoceros isn't white. In reality, they are both grey. Their colours vary depending on the colour of the mud they bathe in. Different regions have different colours of mud.

Talking with you is so confusing. We can't understand anything!
Yeah! You say that you're white because you're **albino**, but you should be grey like all the other white rhinoceros.

As strict vegetarians, rhinoceros eat leaves and branches of thorny bushes and trees, as well as grass and fruit.

In some regions of Africa, rhinoceros also consume wildebeest dung.

Black rhinoceros are one of the few species that eat thorny vegetation. They crush and swallow thorns as long as 10 centimetres (3.9 inches) in length without any problems.

The black rhinoceros is the only animal capable of crossing a massive bush covered in spikes without any discomfort. Its thick skin protects it from scratches.

The white rhinoceros is the second largest land mammal on Earth, after the elephant. Twice as heavy as the black rhinoceros, the white rhinoceros can weigh up to 3.6 tonnes (4 tons).

The white rhinoceros' head can weigh more than 900 kilograms (1,984 pounds). That's the equivalent of the weight of 12 average men.

The rhinoceros navigates with its nose. Its sense of smell is its most developed sense and one of the best in the animal kingdom.

The rhinoceros cannot see well at distances past 30 metres (98 feet). Furthermore, because its tiny eyes are located at the sides of its head, it must turn its head to look directly in front of it.

Because of its bad vision, the rhinoceros is very unpredictable. When it feels threatened, it will charge without cause, whether it's

at cars or peaceful elephants. Some rhinoceros have even been seen charging into trees and boulders that seemed menacing.

Rhinoceros can charge at a speed of 56 kilometres (35 miles) per hour, which is the same speed that most horses gallop at, though horses can maintain their speed for much longer distances than rhinoceros.

Rhinoceros love water. They are excellent swimmers.

41

Other than during mating season, rhinoceros are generally **solitary** creatures.

While rhinoceros mate, they grunt, head-butt each other, spray urine, defecate, and scatter dung around.

Baby rhinoceros are born without horns. The horns will begin to grow in two to three years.

After being pregnant for approximately 16 months, a female will give birth to only one baby. The baby will nurse for about two years and will only stop once the mother gives birth to the next baby.

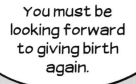

Oxpeckers perch on rhinoceros in order to feed on the rhinoceros' external **parasites**, such as fleas, ticks, and flies. What's more, these birds will fly away when danger approaches, so they serve as watchmen.

The rhinoceros leads a peaceful life and can live for up to 50 years.

Rhinoceros have been hunted for their horns almost to **extinction**. Their horns are sold mainly in Asia.

Rhinoceros are still victims of **poaching** today.

A rhinoceros horn can sell for almost half a million dollars. In some places, the horns are worth more than twice their weight in gold.

In some reserves, we cut off horns in order to protect rhinoceros from poachers.

The rhinoceros is an **endangered** species. There are only about 8,000 individuals left in the world.

Glossary

Albino　a person or animal having an absence of natural colouring in the skin and hair (which is white) and the eyes (which are typically pink)

Endangered　threatened with extinction

Extinction　when a species of plant or animal has died out completely

Keratin　a tough protein that occurs in the outer layer of the skin and in tissues such as nails and hooves

Mammal　a warm-blooded, back-boned animal

Parasite　a creature dependent on another animal for its nutrients and survival

Poaching　the illegal hunting or catching of animals

Rhinoplasty　plastic surgery performed on the nose

Solitary　living alone

Species　a classification of a group of creatures with common characteristics

Index

Do You Know there are other titles?

Rats

Crows

Crocodiles

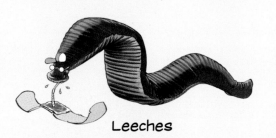

Leeches

Chameleons

Toads

Spiders